This book belongs to:

_____

NATURE NOTEBOOK

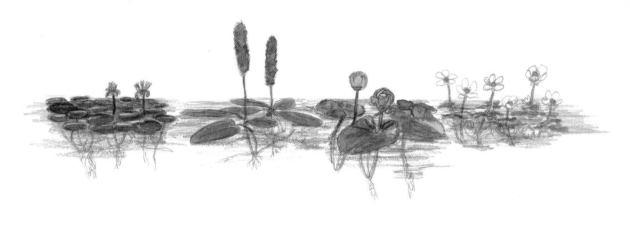

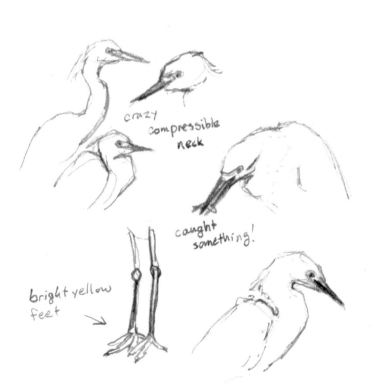

crazy
compressible
neck

caught
something!

bright yellow
feet

tadpole
becoming a frog

folded legs

funny toes!

frog eggs!
stuck to a stick
underwater

reeds grow so close
together I wonder if
their roots are all
entangled

frozen ice in
the stream
reminds me of
a giant glacial
valley

snow drifts
look so much like
sand dunes –
different material
but similar shapes

snowball
fight?

fuzzy

bees seem to like
these flowers

ball of pollen on legs!

cumulus - white, puffy - remind me of the tropics.

stratus clouds are responsible for those flat, overcast skies.

cumulonimbus -
Storm cloud !

cirrus clouds form way high up
and are shaped by the wind.

← love the pointy black crest!

found a blue feather with black bars - from a Steller's jay

bathtime!

I think these are
rabbit footprints!

big strong
back feet

fuzzy ear

I hardly have time to pick up my
pencil from the paper as I draw—
rabbits move fast!

— pointy, slender
leaves

— these irises grow in
tall skinny bunches

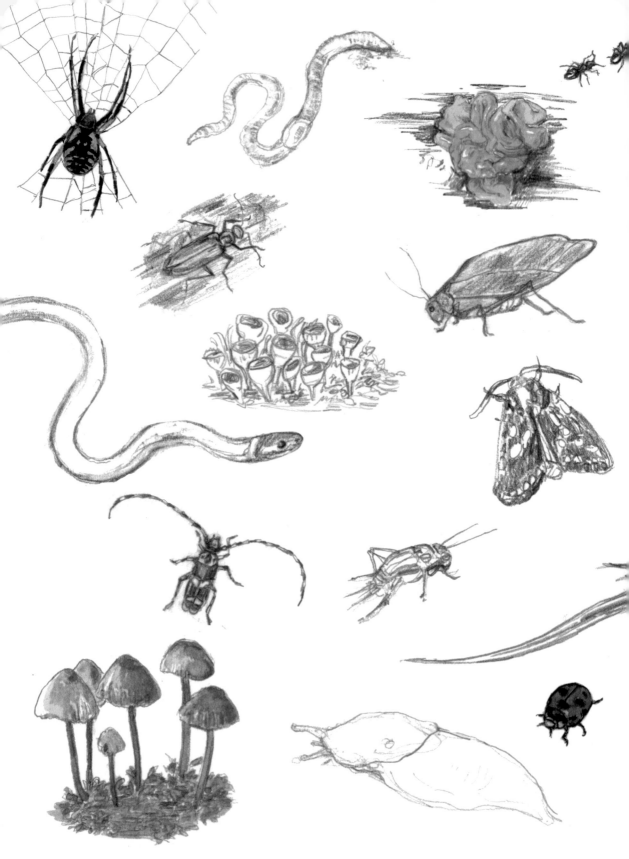

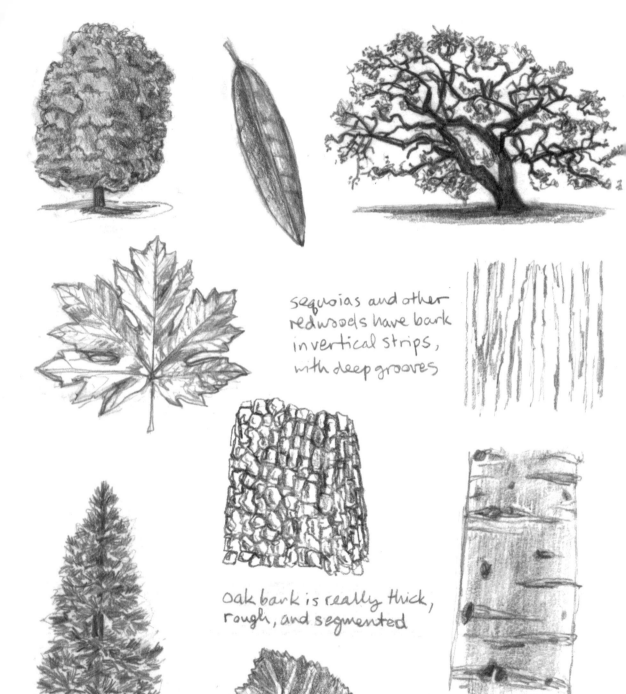

sequoias and other
redwoods have bark
in vertical strips,
with deep grooves

Oak bark is really thick,
rough, and segmented

trees like birch are so
smooth to the touch, with
the thinnest, papery skin
covering them

juveniles of a few local
skink species have these
bright blue tails!